THE HELP! I'M A PARENT HANDBOOK

THE HELP! I'M A PARENT HANDBOOK

A Twelve-Week Program for Raising Better-Behaved, Happier Children

DR. BRUCE NARRAMORE

ZondervanPublishingHouse

Grand Rapids, Michigan

A Division of HarperCollinsPublishers

The Help! I'm a Parent Handbook
Copyright © 1995 by Bruce Narramore

Requests for information should be addressed to:
Zondervan Publishing House
Grand Rapids, Michigan 49530

ISBN: 0-310-30323-0

Edited by Rachel Boers

Printed in the United States of America

95 96 97 98 99 00 01 02 / ❖ DH / 10 9 8 7 6 5 4 3 2 1

CONTENTS

CHAPTER 1

How to Use this Guide

A friend of mine says no one should attempt to rear a child without:

- two dozen guardian angels who carry beepers and never sleep.
- eyes in the back, side, and top of your head.
- a cleaning product that removes peanut butter from carpets, pets, rugs, and walls.
- the patience of Job.
- the wisdom of Solomon (and—if that's lacking—a lie detector to tell you when kids are lying).
- some really catchy phrases like "That's not a threat, that's a promise," "If you do that once more . . .," and "This hurts me more than it hurts you."
- a supply of guilt-inducing comments like "How many times do I have to tell you?" "What's the matter with you anyway?" and "After all I've done for you . . . ."
- some sob stories about how rough you had it when you were a child ("I walked five miles back and forth to school, uphill both ways").
- a friend who tells you that you are doing it all wrong and are about to ruin your children for life.

While some of these really would come in handy (I especially like the lie detector), you can actually rear happy, reasonably well-behaved children with a much shorter list. All you really need is:

- a loving commitment to be a successful parent.
- a way of understanding your children—especially their needs and the reasons they act and feel the way they do.
- a plan or a method for disciplining and meeting their emotional needs.
- practice.
- encouragement and support.

You must *want* to be a loving, helpful mother or father or you wouldn't be starting this parenting program. Along with the principles and techniques in its companion, *Help! I'm a Parent*, *Revised Edition*, the activities in this handbook will give you a way of understanding your children, a practical plan for disciplining effectively and for meeting your children's needs, and practice in applying proven child-rearing techniques. If you are willing to invest a few hours reading and applying this material, I assure you that things will change around your home. I have seen parents solve years of messy rooms, mealtime madness, and homework hassles in a few weeks—sometimes in a matter of days. These principles and techniques aren't radical or complex, they just take a little practice.

Each chapter of this handbook is arranged in three easy-to-understand sections: Review, Application, and Practice. (I call it the RAP method of learning!) **Review** sections summarize the most important points from the corresponding chapter of *Help! I'm a Parent*. **Application** sections show how these principles and techniques work with typical childhood problems. **Practice** sections help you implement the principles and techniques where they really count—with *your* children's sibling fights, undone chores, and other irritating attitudes and actions.

I suggest you complete these exercises with your spouse and/or a few friends. Read the companion chapter in *Help! I'm a Parent*, then complete the handbook exercises. When you finish a chapter, go over your answers with your friends to see how things are working. Nothing will reassure you as much that your children are basically normal than hearing about the similarities in your friends' children! And no one can help you feel as understood and encouraged as other parents who have already been there with their children.

One chapter every week or two is probably the ideal schedule. If you go much faster you will not have time to study your children's behavior and apply your new methods. A longer period between lessons is fine, but it is easy to lose momentum if too much time goes by.

As you go through this program you will come across an occasional page titled **Points for Parents**. These pages summarize some very important concepts. You should note them carefully—perhaps even write out the ideas that apply specifically to your family and post them on your refrigerator or bulletin board where they can serve as a daily reminder or quick reference.

A formal study group at your home or church can work well with this material too. You might even want to organize the group or lead it yourself. This program doesn't require an expert, and you don't have to have a teacher. The activities will move you step by step through a workable approach to parenting so that all you need to do is coordinate the group activities and discussions. If you want to start a study group, the following section gives a few guidelines for groups. If you are just going to do this program by yourself or with your spouse and one or two friends, you can skip the guidelines section and start immediately at chapter 2.

GUIDELINES FOR GROUPS

This handbook was written with classes and study groups in mind as well as individuals. If you cover approximately one chapter each week, for example, you can complete this handbook in a thirteen-week Sunday school class. If you take one or two chapters each meeting you can cover the handbook in a monthly mothers' study group or an evening couples class during the nine months of a school year. Here are a few suggestions if you decide to lead a study group:

- During each meeting, work on parts of two *Handbook* chapters. Begin by having members share their successes and and failures in implementing the Practice sections from the previous week's lesson.
- Then take a few minutes to briefly review the major points of the chapter of *Help! I'm a Parent* that was assigned to be read prior to meeting.
- Use the next part of each meeting to complete the Applications sections of the Handbook that corresponds to the reading assignment of *Help! I'm a Parent*. These sections lend themselves to a class setting. Discuss the applications first and then complete them.
- Assign the Practice exercises from the chapter to be implemented during the coming week.
- Encourage everyone to participate by calling on quiet group members. Ask each person in turn to give their answer to one of the application questions or to relate their experience with a practice exercise. Have members share specific examples of their successes and failures in applying the principles and techniques.
- Be positive and complimentary when group members are sharing.
- If one person tries to dominate the conversation, thank him for his comments and say something like, "Now let's hear what Teresa has tried."
- Maintain the attitude that the Bible is your ultimate authority. Encourage members to share relevant Scripture passages and principles.

My prayers and best wishes are with you. God has given you precious children, and I am confident that if you apply these principles they will help your children grow up in the way that he intends.

CHAPTER 2

Children Misbehave
When Their Needs Aren't Met

REVIEW

None of your children's misbehaviors are "purely accidental." Every irritating habit, every forgotten chore, every upsetting action has a cause. Once you understand these causes you are on your way to effective, lasting discipline. This chapter helps you understand six of the main reasons children misbehave. Chapter 3 covers the other major causes of your children's problem attitudes and actions.

The first six causes of misbehavior lie in unmet emotional needs. God creates every child with four basic emotional needs:

- The need to feel loved
- The need to feel confident
- The need to feel significant and worthwhile
- The need to be involved in interesting, constructive activities

Children misbehave when:

- they are searching for attention because they temporarily feel unloved or left out.
- they are trying to gain power or control because they lack confidence and feel weak and helpless.
- they are trying to be perfect because they feel unworthy or bad about themselves.
- they are turning to some exciting but destructive activity because they are bored.
- they are trying to gain revenge or get even with those who have made them feel unloved, incompetent, unworthy, or bored.
- they are trying to find emotional safety and avoid bad feelings because they have given up hope of feeling loved, competent, or worthy.

11

APPLICATION I

Which of the above six causes are probably behind the following childish misbehaviors? If you think a misbehavior has more than one cause, list the causes in order of importance.

1. An eleven-year-old "smart alec" who constantly disrupts his class.

2. An excessively boy-crazy teenage girl who is deeply hurt when rejected by the opposite sex.

3. A teenager who feels depressed and is constantly belittling herself.

4. A two-year-old who refuses to be toilet trained.

5. A teenager who "accidentally" breaks a glass after being forced to wash the dishes.

6. A quiet ten-year-old who has few friends and seems afraid to seek new friendships.

7. A child who throws a temper tantrum.

8. An excessively competitive child who feels he always has to win.

9. A teenage girl who becomes pregnant in order to spite her parents.

10. A child who refuses to go to bed when asked.

APPLICATION II

Four-year-old Jordan has become increasingly babylike in the past year. He cries often, clings to his mother when she is around, and occasionally has "accidents" at preschool even though he has been toilet trained for well over a year. Jordan's mother and dad both have full-time jobs, and Jordan has a baby brother.

1. Why do you think Jordan has become more babylike?

2. What God-given need may not be sufficiently met in Jordan's life? Why hasn't this need been met?

3. What substitute goal is Jordan turning to?

4. What might Jordan's parents do to help him?

APPLICATION III

You can save yourself a lot of grief by helping your children feel loved, confident, and worthy so they won't have to misbehave to find substitute fulfillment in life. Select one of the three God-given needs listed at the beginning of this chapter and list five things that can undermine that need.

PRACTICE

Select two of your children's behaviors that you would like to change. Describe each behavior, then decide which God-given needs they are trying to meet by turning to a substitute. Decide if they may also be looking for revenge or psychological safety.

First behavior:

> God-given need:
>
> Substitute goal:
>
> Is he also searching for revenge or safety? If so, how?

Second behavior:

> God-given need:
>
> Substitute goal:
>
> Is he also searching for revenge or safety? If so, how?

SCRIPTURE: And my God will meet all your needs according to his glorious riches in Christ Jesus (Philippians 4:19).

PRAYER/MEDITATION: Lord, give me the sensitivity to see beneath my children's misbehaviors to their hurts and needs. Help me to meet those needs so they won't need to misbehave to try to fill a void in their lives.

POINTS FOR PARENTS
Why Children Misbehave

God-Given Emotional Need	Substitute Goal or Counterfeit Satisfaction	Reaction to Frustrated Needs and Goals
Love	Attention	Anger or Revenge and Search for Psychological Safety
Confidence	Power and Control	
Worth	Perfection	
Constructive Activity	Destructive Activity	

CHAPTER 3

Kids Will Be Kids

REVIEW

Not all childish misbehavior stems from unmet needs; some irritating habits are caused by our children's inherited temperaments or personalities. Some children are "slow to warm up"—they just aren't as outgoing and excited about new activities, new friends, and new foods as other children. "Easy" children are more relaxed and adaptable; they don't mind changes in their routines and are friendly and even-tempered. "Difficult" children have a harder time adapting from the day they are born. As babies they are more intense and easily upset, they sleep and eat irregularly, kick and scream more, and are bothered by noises that their brothers and sisters hardly notice.

In addition, some things children do that bug parents the most are caused by normal childishness. Infants are supposed to cry, toddlers are supposed to get messy and dirty, five-year-olds are supposed to ask questions, eight-year-old boys are supposed to hang out together and "hate" girls, and teenagers are supposed to go through at least one phase of argumentativeness or negativity. As upsetting as these things may be to us, they aren't misbehaviors in the sense that they represent some abnormality or unmet need. It's just the way kids are.

Children whose normal developmental traits or inborn personalities cause irritation for others in the family may need training and discipline just like children who are misbehaving because of unmet needs. But as you train them, let them know you value their special style at the same time you help them rein it in just a bit.

On top of unique temperaments and normal developmental stages, children also have a sinful or selfish tendency. In some way, at some times, all children want their own way. They want to be the first, the best, the most loved, the strongest, or the best looking in their family, class, or circle of friends. They want to win instead of lose, and they prefer not to do their chores and not to share.

Since children's misbehaviors result from a combination of their inborn temperament, their sinful nature, their developmental stage, and their unmet emotional needs, it's important to know which of these motivations is causing your children to get in trouble. Let's review the nine main reasons children misbehave:

- They are searching for attention because they are temporarily feeling unloved or left out.
- They are trying to gain power or control because they lack confidence and feel weak and helpless.
- They are trying to be perfect because they feel unworthy or bad about themselves.
- They are bored, so they are turning to some exciting, but destructive activity.
- They are trying to gain revenge or get even with those who have made them feel unloved, incompetent, unworthy, or bored.
- They are trying to find emotional safety and avoid feeling unloved, incompetent, unworthy, or bored because they have given up hope.
- They are acting like a normal child their age.
- They are reflecting their own distinctive personality.
- They are acting on the tendency of all people to be selfish and sinful.

APPLICATION I

Some of the following behaviors are normal actions for a child of that age. Some reflect the child's distinctive personality style or temperament. Others are caused by the child's innate tendency to be selfish or sinful. Still others stem from the unmet emotional needs we discussed in chapter 2. Identify which actions are *normal*, which ones reflect your child's *temperament*, which ones are caused their *innate selfish tendencies* and which ones stem from *unmet needs*. If some of the behaviors seem to be caused by more than one of these, list the likely causes in order of their probable significance.

1. A two-year-old who always says "No."

2. A nine-year-old "smart alec" who repeatedly acts up in class.

3. A finicky eater who picks at his food.

4. A three-year-old who asks, "Why? Why? Why? Why?"

5. A teenage girl who won't let her younger sister wear her clothes.

6. A teenager who has few friends, seriously overeats, and often secludes herself in her room to read romance novels.

7. A seven-year-old who fidgets at a wedding.

8. A teenage girl who seems excessively "boy crazy."

9. A baby who kicks and cries while his diaper is being changed.

10. A child whose room always looks like a tornado just hit it.

PRACTICE I

Select one of your children's behaviors that is normal for his or her age or a result of his or her special temperament. Then answer the questions below.

Behavior:

1. How do you feel when your child acts that way?

2. Does this normal action bother you? Why?

3. Now that you realize this is normal, what can you do to not overreact? (Hints: Ignore it, count to ten, see the humor or creativity in it, decide to let God teach you patience, etc.)

4. If your child needs some guidance or training with this behavior, even though it's normal or just part of his personality style, what training or help might you give him?

5. Commit yourself to responding differently to this behavior for one week. At the end of the week, write down the changes in yourself and your child.

PRACTICE II

Select one of your children's misbehaviors that seems to reflect a sinful or selfish tendency. Write down that misbehavior and answer the questions that follow.

Misbehavior:

1. Since most misbehaviors reflect a mixture of our children's sinfulness, their unmet God-given needs, their unique personalities, and their normal developmental reactions, estimate what percent of this action is caused by each of these factors.

   Sinfulness or selfishness   ____
   Unmet God-given needs   ____
   Unique personality   ____
   Normal developmental stage   ____
   Total   <u>100%</u>

2. Write out what you can do to address each part of the problem.

Sinfulness or selfishness:

Unmet God-given needs:

Unique personality:

Normal developmental stage:

❧

SCRIPTURE: When I was a child, I talked like a child, I thought like a child, I reasoned like a child. When I became a man, I put childish ways behind me (1 Corinthians 13:11).

PRAYER/MEDITATION: Lord, help me not to squelch or try to change what should be nurtured in my child. Help me parent my children as the unique people you have created them to be rather than try to change them because of my own low tolerance. Help me tell the difference between problems caused by their unique style, my failure to meet their needs, and their own sinfulness or self-centeredness.

Discipline or Punishment?

REVIEW

Children need discipline, but that is very different from punishment. Discipline is carried out by fathers and mothers who want to help their children grow, while punishment is dispensed by a judge to make offenders suffer for their crime. Punishment focuses on past misbehaviors, while discipline focuses on future, correct behaviors. And punishment is done more to vent our anger or get even with our children, while discipline is done in love. Just as God never punishes his children, we should never punish ours. Discipline may be firm and even painful, but it should always be carried out in love. Let's review the key points from chapter 4 of *Help! I'm a Parent*:

- Much of our parenting can be modeled after God's training of his children.
- God disciplines his children, but he never punishes.
- The purpose of punishment is justice and revenge.
- The purpose of discipline is to train for maturity and for the child's best interest.
- Punishment is carried out in anger, whereas discipline is done in love.
- Punishment creates fear, guilt, and anger in children.
- Fear, guilt, and anger are poor motivators and create untold emotional problems.
- Children need to learn to respect others and to be aware of the negative consequences of their actions, but respect is entirely different from fear.

APPLICATION I

The following passage gives an example of God's discipline. Read it and answer the questions that follow.

The teachers of the law and the Pharisees brought in a woman caught in adultery. They made her stand before the group and said to Jesus, "Teacher, this woman was caught in the act of adultery. In the Law Moses commanded us to stone such women. Now what do you say?" They were using this question as a trap, in order to have a basis for accusing him. But Jesus bent down and started to write on the ground with his finger. When they kept on questioning him, he straightened up and said to them, "If any one of you is without sin, let him be the first to throw a stone at her." Again he stooped down and wrote on the ground. At this, those who heard began to go away one at a time, the older ones first, until only Jesus was left, with the woman still standing there. Jesus straightened up and asked her, "Woman, where are they? Has no one condemned you?" "No one, sir," she said. "Then neither do I condemn you," Jesus declared. "Go now and leave your life of sin."

JOHN 8:3–11

1. What was Jesus' attitude toward the leaders who wanted to punish the adulterous woman?

2. What was Jesus' attitude toward the woman?

3. What was Jesus' purpose in speaking with the woman caught in adultery?

4. Did Jesus focus on the woman's past or her future?

5. How do you think the woman felt after her encounter with Jesus?

6. Do you think the woman changed her adulterous behavior? Why or why not?

APPLICATION II

Think of an instance when your parents punished you in anger instead of disciplining you in love. Then answer the questions below.

Your misbehavior:

1. How did you feel about yourself?

2. How did you feel toward your parents?

3. Did your behavior change permanently or only temporarily?

4. How long did it take to restore your good feelings about yourself and toward your parents?

PRACTICE I

Think of two times you corrected your children recently—once when you disciplined, and once when you punished. Then answer the following questions.

Punishment

1. What was your child's misbehavior?

2. How did you feel when you saw what she had done?

3. What was your tone of voice when you punished her?

4. What was your purpose in punishment?

5. What was your child's response—her words, actions, and apparent feelings?

6. How might you have reacted differently?

7. Did you apologize to your child later? If so, how did she respond?

Discipline

1. What was your child's misbehavior?

2. How did you feel when you saw what he had done?

3. What was your tone of voice when you disciplined him?

4. What was your purpose in disciplining?

5. What was your child's response—his words, actions, and apparent feelings?

6. How did you feel about yourself and your child after disciplining him?

PRACTICE II

Select one thing your child does that really makes you angry and for which you tend to punish instead of discipline. (Hint: Choose the one that makes your child think, *If I really want to see Mom or Dad lose it, I just . . .*)

Misbehavior:

1. How do you feel when your child acts this way?

2. Why do you think this particular misbehavior upsets you so much?

3. Would you be willing to covenant with God and a friend to learn to react to your child more lovingly the next time you need to discipline him for this action?

4. Assuming you are committed to learning to discipline in love, plan a new strategy that you can implement the next time he acts this way. You may decide to discipline him when he first begins to misbehave, before things get out of hand. Or you may decide to count to one hundred, call a friend, or let your spouse handle the situation. Write your plan here.

5. Implement your plan during the coming week. Then write down how it worked and the difference it made for both you and your child.

6. If you need to modify your plan or keep working on part of it, write that below.

SCRIPTURE: We have all had human fathers who disciplined us and we respected them for it. How much more should we submit to the Father of our spirits and live! Our fathers disciplined us for a little while as they thought best; but God disciplines us for our good, that we may share in his holiness (Hebrews 12:9–10).

PRAYER/MEDITATION: Lord, help me to be quick to listen and understand, but slow to speak and slow to anger (James 1:19). Help me to understand the impact that words spoken in anger can have on my children and help me to learn self-control (Proverbs 17:27).

POINTS FOR PARENTS
Punishment and Discipline

	Punishment	Discipline
Purpose	To inflict penalty for an offense (Matt. 25:46)	To train for correction and maturity (Heb. 12:5–11)
Focus	Past misdeeds (2 Thess. 1:7–9)	Future correct deeds (Prov. 3:11–12)
Parent's Attention	Hostility and frustration on the part of the parent (Isa. 13:9–11)	Love and concern on the part of the parent (Rev. 3:19)
Message the Child Hears	You are bad. I dislike you. You deserve to suffer.	Because I care for you, I must do this to help you learn.
Resulting Behavior in the Child	Conformity or rebellion	Growth (Titus 2:1–14)
Resulting Emotion in the Child	Fear, guilt or hostility (Heb. 12:18–21)	Security (Heb. 12:22–24; 1 John 4:18–19)

CHAPTER 5

Three Tools for Toddler Taming and Child Training

REVIEW

Children learn behaviors that are rewarded and unlearn actions that are not rewarded. Even behaviors that begin out of the misguided search for attention, power, or perfectionism are only continued if your children receive some type of reward for their efforts. If your son misbehaves to gain attention but doesn't get it, he will eventually stop misbehaving. And if your daughter throws a tantrum to get her way and you don't give in, she'll stop throwing tantrums. Here are the main principles that determine which behaviors your children will learn and maintain:

- Actions that are rewarded are more likely to be repeated in the future.
- Behaviors that are not rewarded tend to weaken and disappear.
- A reward is anything that satisfies a child's goal or leads to pleasure.
- Rewards work best when they come soon after the desired behavior.
- Parents often unknowingly reward undesirable actions even though we don't approve of the behavior (e.g., when we give in to their whining, it's likely our children will whine again the next time they don't get their way).
- Children also reward *our* undesirable behaviors (e.g., if they do what we want after we remind them a dozen times, we are more likely to nag and remind them next time).
- Children learn by imitating us.

APPLICATION

In the following examples, see how you might be rewarding your children for the very behaviors you wish they would stop.

1. You have just told your son he is not allowed to have candy before supper. He cries hysterically, and you can't stand the noise. Finally you say, "Okay, but just this once."

How did you reinforce your son's crying?

What is likely to happen next time you tell him he may not have candy?

2. Your twelve-year-old spontaneously helps clear the supper dishes. You say, "Thanks for clearing the table, Heather. Since I'm through with dishes early, let's go to the mall and look for that new outfit you've been wanting for school."

   How did you reward your daughter's positive behavior?

   What is more likely to happen tomorrow night after supper?

3. You are sitting quietly on the couch when your ten-year-old daughter yells, "Mother, he hit me!" "Stop it, Peter," you scold. "You know better than that!"

   What motivation probably prompted Peter to hit his sister?

   Did you reinforce that behavior? If so, how?

   What is likely to happen the next time Peter wants attention?

4. As you walk downtown, your daughter continually lags behind. You tell her to hurry, but then stop and wait until she finally catches up.

   How are you reinforcing her lagging?

What could you do that would not reward her lagging and would extinguish this undesirable behavior?

PRACTICE

Pick one behavior you would like to change by using the principles of reinforcement and extinction. Whining, temper tantrums, and mealtime misconduct usually respond well to these methods of training. Don't start with more than one behavior; if you try to change several things at once, it won't work. It is also important to be specific. "Improve Johnny's table manners" is too vague. Instead, pick something like, "I want to teach Johnny to say 'please' every time he asks for something" or "I want Johnny to stop kicking his sister under the table."

Now for the bad news. When you first apply any new principle, your child may test you. If you decide to extinguish temper tantrums by ignoring them, you should expect the next tantrum to be the loudest ever! Your child is losing a powerful weapon and won't give up until he is convinced you are going to stick to your guns. Also, be consistent. Once you decide to ignore a misbehavior, you must ignore it every time. Inconsistent discipline will actually *increase* the likelihood of tantrums!

With these warnings, let's begin. Follow the steps below and watch the results.

1. Describe the specific behavior you want to eliminate.

2. Sometimes it is important to know just how bad a problem is before starting a new discipline. For a period of one week before starting the new discipline, carefully record the frequency of the behavior you have chosen to change.

Number of Misbehaviors

	Sunday	Monday	Tuesday	Wednesday	Thursday	Friday	Saturday
8							
7							
6							
5							
4							
3							
2							
1							

3. When a misbehavior is a simple habit (like not saying please or failing to do homework), taking away rewards for negative behaviors and rewarding positive ones is often all you need to do. But in case the problem is caused by unmet emotional needs, it isn't wise to simply ignore that behavior. If your daughter misbehaves to gain attention because she feels unloved, don't just ignore her. First do all you can to meet her God-given need for love and *then* ignore (extinguish) her attention-getting misbehavior.

Are you neglecting any of the four God-given needs, thus causing the misbehavior? If so, which need(s) are you neglecting?

How can you meet the neglected God-given need(s) so that your child won't feel she has to turn to misbehavior?

4. Assuming you are now doing all you can to meet your child's God-given needs, the next step is to eliminate rewards for the negative behavior. List the rewards your child has been receiving.

5. The final step in changing behavior is to reinforce a positive behavior that competes with the undesirable action. When a child says "Please pass the butter" in a pleasant voice, he can't be saying "Gimme that" at the same time. By rewarding politeness, you eliminate impoliteness. What competing, positive behavior can you reward? How?

6. The day you begin the new procedures of extinction and reward, start a new weekly behavior chart. Record each occurrence of the undesired behavior so you can compare it with the first chart and see the improvement.

Number of Misbehaviors

	Sunday	Monday	Tuesday	Wednesday	Thursday	Friday	Saturday
8							
7							
6							
5							
4							
3							
2							
1							

Most behaviors begin to change after the first few days of discipline, but deeply entrenched habits may take weeks to alter. Remember to be consistent. If you don't see progress after two weeks, reevaluate your method by asking these four questions:

1. Are there still emotional needs for love, confidence, worth, or constructive activities that must be met before the problem is solved?

2. Is my child getting rewards from me (such as attention or revenge) for her misconduct that I didn't recognize?

3. Are the rewards I am using to encourage desirable behavior things my child finds rewarding? If not, what better rewards can I use?

4. Am I or my spouse perhaps modeling the very thing I'm trying to change in my child?

If rewards and extinction don't solve the problem, your child may need some natural or logical consequences. But don't forget these learning principles, because all good discipline begins here. Spankings, natural and logical consequences, and other types of discipline won't work if your child is still being rewarded for misbehavior.

SCRIPTURE: Train a child in the way he should go, and when he is old he will not turn from it (Proverbs 22:6).

PRAYER/MEDITATION: Lord, my children's habits are learned. Help me be part of the solution instead of part of the problem. Remind me to reward their positive habits and not their negative ones, and help me to be a good example.

CHAPTER 6

Let Nature Discipline Your Child

REVIEW

Many misbehaviors have painful natural consequences. If children don't eat, they become hungry. If they touch a hot stove, they burn their fingers. If they throw their toys, the toys may break. As long as the natural consequences of a misbehavior won't cause severe or lasting damage, you can let your children learn a few lessons from the school of hard knocks. Natural consequences have three advantages over most other forms of discipline:

- They eliminate parent-child power struggles. Instead of warning, nagging, threatening, and reminding our children, we let the built-in consequences teach them a lesson.
- They teach children to take responsibility for their actions. Once we stop reminding them, they have to remember for themselves or suffer the consequence.
- They teach children to respect us and our advice. When things turn out the way we predicted, children pay closer attention the next time we speak.

APPLICATION I

Jillian was the champion procrastinator of the sixth grade. After years of helping Jillian rush through her homework at the last minute, her mom finally told her that the next time she put off her homework until the last minute, she would not stay up late to help her. Sure enough, when Jillian "forgot" to finish a book report, her mom told her she was sorry Jillian had forgotten, but that she was going to bed. As she lay in bed she heard Jillian crying.

1. What should Jillian's mom do?

   a. Angrily tell Jillian, "I've warned you a hundred times. You got yourself into this mess. It's up to you to get yourself out."

   b. Lay in bed feeling badly but reminding herself that this is really for Jillian's good.

   c. Get up and tell Jillian, "Okay, but this is absolutely, positively the last time I will do this. Now, *Moby Dick* is the story of a big white whale and a man named . . ."

   d. Look for the Cliff Notes she used when she was in school.

2. If Jillian was your daughter, could you stay in bed even if she cried? Why or why not?

APPLICATION II

Ten-year-old Rebekah leaves her dirty clothes all over her room. Although her mother regularly reminds her to put them in the dirty clothes basket, Rebekah keeps "forgetting." When she is of clean clothes, she runs to her mother and asks her to drop whatever she is doing to wash a load of clothes. Since Rebekah's mother is getting tired of washing clothes two or three times a week, let's give her a little help.

1. How can Rebekah's mother use a natural consequence to motivate Rebekah to put her dirty clothes in the hamper?

2. How will Rebekah probably respond the first time her mother sticks to the natural consequence?

Every winter, Rebekah's brother Todd argues with their mother that he doesn't need to wear warm clothes.

1. Whose problem is it that Todd doesn't want to wear warm clothes?

2. Why do you think Todd's mom stays in this power struggle with her son?

3. If Todd really does need to wear warmer clothes, what's the best way for him to find out for himself?

APPLICATION III

Sometimes the lessons we learn in the school of hard knocks stay with us the longest. Write down one childhood lesson you learned from suffering the natural consequences of your own actions and tell why that lesson worked for you.

APPLICATION IV

What natural consequence will teach each of these children a lesson if Mom and Dad warn them once and then let them suffer the consequences?

1. A boy who "forgets" his school lunch or his lunch money.

2. A girl who wants to touch her mother's hot curling iron.

3. A teenager who spends her entire allowance on CDs.

4. A teenager who drives faster than the speed limit.

5. A child who wears a weird-looking shirt.

6. A boy who tilts back in his chair.

7. A child who doesn't do his homework.

8. A teenager who doesn't fill the car with gas before a date.

PRACTICE I

Natural consequences work especially well for children who don't eat well, get up on time, dress warmly, or generally fail to take responsibility for their bodies and their property. Anytime your children's actions could cause damage or loss of their own property or pain to their bodies, you probably don't need to look for other methods of discipline.

How would your child complete the following phrase: "Oh, I never have to take responsibility to _____ . My mom will remind me"?

1. What natural consequence could probably motivate your child to stop that behavior if you let him suffer the consequence?

2. What has kept you from letting that consequence train your child until now?

3. Put this simple five-step plan to work:
   • Tell your child that you will no longer nag or remind him.
   • Tell him once of the potential natural consequence.
   • Get out of the way and let the consequence work.
   • When the painful consequence comes, be sympathetic.
   • If he tries to make you feel guilty, don't give in.

If you are in a class or group, break into pairs and role-play the conversation that might take place when you explain this new method of discipline to your child. Don't give in, no matter how many excuses or how much whining the role-playing child does. *Note to friend*: Be merciless! *Note to parent*: Be strong!

1. After one week, write out the results of your allowing your child to suffer the consequence for his behavior.

2. How does it feel to get out of the power struggle and let your child take responsibility for this part of his life?

PRACTICE II

Some consequences are too dangerous or lasting, and sometimes the natural consequence is delayed too long. The consequence of not brushing your teeth, for example, is so delayed that it won't motivate most children. The potential consequence of letting toddlers play in the street is too severe. List five of your children's actions for which natural consequences aren't appropriate. The next chapter will explain how to handle these behaviors.

1.

2.

3.

4.

5.

SCRIPTURE: Do not be deceived: God cannot be mocked. A man reaps what he sows (Galatians 6:7).

PRAYER: Lord, give me the courage to let my children suffer a little pain now so they can learn some big lessons for later in life. And help my children know that I am letting them experience the consequences of their own actions because I love them and want them to take responsibility for their lives.

CHAPTER 7

Logical Consequences:
You *Can* Teach Children to Obey

Medical Alert: An epidemic of hearing loss and memory lapse in children is sweeping the country. If untreated, the children worsen until they cause near insanity in parents. Universal symptoms include children saying "I forget" and "I didn't hear you call." So far, only one remedy is known—logical consequences administered in consistent doses.

REVIEW

When life doesn't provide a built-in painful consequence, a logical consequence can be used to improve our children's hearing and their memory. The difference between natural and logical consequences is that with logical consequences we structure our own discipline to teach our children a lesson, but with natural consequences the painful result is built into the act itself. Like natural consequences, logical consequences work because children will change their behavior once they suffer enough painful consequences.

Logical consequences work miracles with chores and responsibilities around the house. If your daughter forgets to feed her pet, simply tell her, "We each have responsibilities. I feed the people and you feed the animals. If you don't feed Fido, you will have to miss dinner." If your son is consistently late for meals, don't allow him to eat any dinner unless he arrives on time. These consequences may seem severe at first, but remember, you are not punishing your children or trying to hurt them. Instead, you are teaching them to take responsibility for their actions by letting them suffer a fitting consequence. A couple of missed meals are a small price to pay if they will help you rid yourself of years of frenzied routine and teach your children to take responsibility for their own actions.

APPLICATION I

Read the following paragraph to learn how Mark and Holly got out of a long-standing power struggle and taught their twelve-year-old son to take responsibility for his bedwetting:

One thing has been driving us up the wall: Jason is twelve and still wetting the bed. His doctor has tried medication and other things, but nothing works. He has periods when he is dry for a few days and then he'll do it every single night. It seems like he doesn't care at all. We finally told him that if his bed was wet, he would have to wash and change his sheets before he left the house. The first time it happened it took him until eleven in the morning. We had to leave, and by the time we got back it was done. The bed hasn't been wet since.

1. Of the eight basic motivations for our children's actions, which two were probably causing Jason's bedwetting?

2. The best answer to the previous question is probably attention. By manipulating his mom into changing his sheets, Jason got her attention. She showed concern, talked to him, and even drove him to the doctor. Each of these actions rewarded his attention-getting behavior. Jason's bedwetting may also have been caused by anger and a search for power or for revenge. He may have resented his younger sibling, who was getting more attention. If that's the case, his bedwetting served the dual purpose of gaining attention and punishing his mother for the attention he lost to his younger sibling. If these were the dynamics, how would making him change his own sheets stop his bedwetting?* (The answer can be found below, but please try to answer on your own first.)

3. If Jason was wetting the bed to get attention, would having him wash his own sheets solve his internal emotional problem? Why or why not?

*ANSWER: Since Holly stopped giving Jason extra attention, he lost the rewards he had been receiving for bedwetting. Since he had to change his own sheets, he was also no longer getting revenge on his mother; he was only hurting himself.

4. What else would Mark and Holly need to do to be most helpful to Jason?

APPLICATION II

List some logical consequences for the following, making sure to think of a discipline that fits the action.

1. Not getting to dinner on time:

2. Not washing the car:

3. Leaving a school report until the last minute:

4. Leaving athletic equipment on the living room floor:

5. Failing to clean a room:

6. "Forgetting" to practice the piano:

7. Playing music too loud:

8. Fighting with a sibling:

PRACTICE

Now it's time to apply logical consequences to *your* children. Pick two misbehaviors that are threatening your sanity and that might be altered by using logical consequences. Make sure it's a specific problem, such as being late for school or failing to carry out the trash. Then complete the following:

First misbehavior:

1. What method of discipline have you been using?

2. Has it worked? Why or why not?

3. What logical consequence could you utilize to teach your child better behavior?

4. How did your child react when you communicated your plan to her and explained that it will be up to her to decide whether she will do the desired thing or suffer the consequence?

5. Describe what happens the next time your child engages in that misbehavior. (It may take a few applications of a consequence to change the behavior, so be sure you consistently apply the consequence and avoid power struggles.)

Second misbehavior:

1. What method of discipline have you been using?

2. Has it worked? Why or why not?

3. What logical consequence could you utilize to teach your child better behavior?

4. How did your child react when you communicated your plan to him and explained that it will be up to him to decide whether he will do the desired thing or suffer the consequence?

5. Describe what happens the next time your child engages in that misbehavior. (Again, it may take a few applications of a consequence to change the behavior, so be sure you consistently apply the consequence and avoid power struggles.)

SCRIPTURE: Discipline your son, and he will give you peace; he will bring delight to your soul (Proverbs 29:17).

PRAYER/MEDITATION: Lord, I pray that I will lovingly teach my children to be responsible for their actions. Help me to train and discipline them instead of nag them, and to not let my own fears or guilt keep me from carrying though on the consequences I establish.

CHAPTER 8

To Spank or Not to Spank?

REVIEW

"Spare the rod and spoil the child" was the accepted wisdom in many circles in the first half of this century. More recently, educators and psychologists have challenged the helpfulness of spankings and concluded that many (if not all) spankings are abusive and unnecessary. Some spankings are abusive, but physical discipline can also be a useful training tool if it is used judiciously and appropriately. Here are the basic principles of physical discipline:

- Never spank a child in anger. That is punishment, not discipline, and it causes fear, depression, and resentment.
- Spankings should not be utilized when there is another equally effective method of discipline available.
- If your child is looking for attention or trying to gain revenge by upsetting you, spankings won't work. They may actually reward his misbehavior.
- We should never spank infants, since they don't understand consequences, only that someone they need is hurting them.
- From about age one until four is the most appropriate time for occasional spankings. Once a child is old enough to communicate well and to profit from other measures, spanking should end.
- Spankings don't help meet the emotional needs that cause many childhood misbehaviors. Consequently, the effectiveness of spanking is limited to temporarily controlling behavior—it doesn't help children feel understood or enable them to grow emotionally.

APPLICATION I

Check the behaviors below that might require a spanking or a swat on the hand or bottom.

—— A toddler who keeps getting into her mother's knickknacks.

—— A child who wants to stick a hairpin in an electrical outlet.

—— A teenage boy who sasses his mom.

—— A two-year-old who bites his baby sister.

—— A nine-year-old who won't get dressed in time to go to church.

—— A three-year-old who climbs where he could fall and be severely injured.

—— A thirteen-year-old who refuses to turn off the TV.

We can often avoid spanking if we plan creatively, take some preventive steps, or consider other types of discipline. What might you be able to do instead of spanking in each of the above situations? Write your suggestions in the space after each sentence.*

APPLICATION II

Our attitudes about spanking are influenced by our experiences as children. Did your parents punish or discipline you by spanking? How does that make you feel about spanking your own children?

*ANSWER: I imagine you came up with ideas like "kiddie proofing" your home, putting plastic safety plugs in electrical outlets, talking with your teenager to find out what is bugging him, and perhaps a few logical consequences. I am not suggesting we should never spank, but this exercise shows that we can generally come up with effective alternatives to spanking if we take a little time to think about it.

APPLICATION III

Pretend you are preparing for a debate on the topic "Is all spanking abusive and unnecessary?" Since you don't know which side you will be assigned, prepare arguments for both positions. If you are in a class or study group, divide into groups, prepare your points, and have a fifteen-minute debate. Then list the pros and cons of spanking.

Pros:

Cons:

PRACTICE I

If your child is between one and four years old, use the questions below to evaluate the effectiveness of the last time you spanked her.

Misbehavior:

1. What were your feelings as you spanked your child?

2. How hard and how often did you spank her?

3. What was your child's immediate emotional response?

4. Was the spanking effective in changing the undesirable behavior? If so, for how long?

If the spanking didn't seem to be effective or did not last long, there could be several reasons: a.) there may have been a better method of discipline available, b.) you may have spanked in anger, c.) your child may have been looking for attention and you gave it to him, d.) your spanking may not have hurt, e.) you may not be consistently disciplining for that behavior. Which of these reasons (or others) may have caused the ineffectiveness?

SCRIPTURE: The rod of correction imparts wisdom, but a child left to himself disgraces her mother (Proverbs 29:15).

PRAYER/MEDITATION: Lord, if my child needs physical correction, help me discipline her lovingly yet firmly for her own good. Help me not to punish her to vent my anger or get even with her. And help her to know I love her and respect her deeply even when I discipline her.

CHAPTER 9

Creating a Plan and Making It Work

REVIEW

We have covered six principles or techniques of discipline:

- Extinction
- Reinforcement or rewards
- Modeling
- Natural consequences
- Logical consequences
- Spanking

None of these methods work in every situation. For example, natural consequences help us avoid power struggles, but many of our children's misbehaviors have no immediately painful built-in consequence. Logical consequences generally work great when no natural consequences are available, but there isn't a logical consequence for every action. Spanking may occasionally be helpful with young children when the natural consequence would cause severe or lasting harm to a child and there is no workable logical consequence. The learning principles of rewards, extinction, and imitation are always helpful, but often won't solve problems all by themselves. This chapter will help you select the disciplines or methods that are most appropriate to a specific problem.

POINTS FOR PARENTS
Choosing a Method of Discipline

Method of Discipline	When to Use	Lesson your Child Learns
Reinforcement or Rewards	1. Anytime you want to strengthen a desirable behavior. 2. Especially helpful when teaching new skills or taking new responsibilities.	"When I do the right thing, something good happens. I think I will do that again."
Extinction or removing rewards for misbehavior	1. Anytime you want to weaken undesirable behavior. 2. Especially effective when combined with a reward for a competing postitive behavior.	"When I misbehave, I don't get any reward. There's no sense trying that again."
Modeling or Imitation	1. This method is in continuous operation.	"My parents are strong and grown-up. I want to be like them."
Natural Consequences	1. When you want to weaken undesirable behavior. 2. When the act has a built-in painful result. 3. When children ignore your advice.	"When I do something, I can get hurt. I don't have anyone to blame. I won't do that again!"
Logical Consequences	1. When you want to weaken undesirable behavior. 2. When no natural consequence exists. 3. When natural consequences would cause severe or lasting hurt to the child. 4. When you are being sucked into a power struggle.	"When I do something that is wrong, I penalize myself. I'll do my best to avoid that in the future!"
Spanking	1. When children are at least one year old but too young to profit from other discipline. 2. When we can do it lovingly.	"Ouch. My parents are in charge here. I may not like it but I'm not doing that again."

APPLICATION I

Circle the method(s) of discipline most likely to be successful in the following examples:

1. An eight-year-old who throws a temper tantrum.
   a. Spanking
   b. Communication
   c. Modeling
   d. Extinction
   e. Threat ("I'll give you something to cry about!")

2. A teenager who repeatedly breaks curfew.
   a. Extinction
   b. Spanking
   c. Crying (Make her feel guilty because you feel like a complete failure as a parent)
   d. Logical consequences
   e. Reinforcement

3. A ten-month-old who purposely pours his drink onto the floor after every meal.
   a. Adoption (give the child away!)
   b. Reinforcement
   c. Spanking
   d. Communication
   e. Extinction

4. A child who eats very little at meals and then keeps asking for snacks.
   a. Spanking
   b. Reinforcement
   c. Natural Consequences
   d. Modeling
   e. Get a snack machine and let him earn money to buy his own

5. A four-year-old who repeatedly acts up while you are shopping.
   a. Leave him at the store
   b. Logical Consequences
   c. Spanking

d. Reinforcement

e. Natural Consequences

6. A sloppy child who won't pick up after himself.

   a. Logical consequences

   b. Spanking

   c. Modeling

   d. Nagging longer and louder

7. An eleven-year-old "slowpoke" who can't get going in the mornings.

   a. Reinforcement

   b. Natural consequences

   c. Modeling

   d. Shame her in front of her friends

   e. Extinction (the behavior, not the child!)

8. A child who doesn't come when you call.

   a. Reinforcement

   b. Logical consequences

   c. Extinction

   d. Yell louder

9. A brother and sister who fight all the time.

   a. Spanking

   b. Natural consequences

   c. Reinforcement

   d. Logical consequences

   e. Extinction (let them kill each other!)

10. A three-year-old who disobeys your instruction.

    a. Reinforcement

    b. Spanking

    c. Extinction

    d. Lecture

APPLICATION II

To learn when to use each type of discipline, list the main advantages and disadvantages for each method.

Spankings

Advantages:

Disadvantages:

Natural Consequences

Advantages:

Disadvantages:

Logical Consequences

Advantages:

Disadvantages:

Rewards and Extinction

Advantages:

Disadvantages:

Modeling or Imitation

Advantages:

Disadvantages:

PRACTICE I

We discipline, of course, to change our children's behavior. But that's not the only reason. Helpful discipline enhances our children's self-esteem, builds feelings of security, and helps them become more self-disciplined. Answering the following questions can help you decide how effective your discipline is.

- Did my child's behavior change?
- Did the discipline maintain my child's self-respect?
- Did I keep a loving, sensitive connection with my child as I disciplined?
- Were there any negative side effects of the discipline?
- Did it help my child become more self-disciplined and responsible?

Select a recent time you disciplined your child and use these guidelines to evaluate the effectiveness of your discipline.

Misbehavior:

1. How did you discipline?

2. Did your child's behavior change? If not, why not?

3. Did the discipline maintain your child's self-respect? In what way?

4. Were you able to maintain a sensitive, loving connection with your child as you disciplined? In what way?

5. Were there any negative side effects? If so, what were they?

6. Did the discipline help your child become more responsible and self-disciplined?

7. Do you now see another method that would be more effective? How might that method be more effective?

SCRIPTURE: By wisdom a house is built, and through understanding it is established (Proverbs 24:3).

PRAYER/MEDITATION: Lord, help me to understand my children and to be sensitive to their needs. Teach me how to help them grow and learn and prepare for life. Let me see when they need to suffer the consequences of their actions and when I can help in other ways by listening carefully and offering encouraging words and a good example.

Keeping Your Cool
While Your Children Are Losing Theirs

REVIEW

Angry punishment doesn't work. Even when we get the behavior we want by frightening children with anger, we create other problems. Let's review the major points from chapter 10 of *Help! I'm a Parent!*:

- It is natural to occasionally lose our tempers with our children. That's part of being human.
- There's nothing wrong with feeling angry. Anger only becomes a problem when we impulsively act on it or when we seek revenge or try to hurt our children.
- Mismanaged anger undermines children's self-esteem, frightens them, and erects barriers between us and our children.
- Angry feelings can be managed so that they do not damage children.

This chapter will help you handle your anger more effectively by understanding where anger comes from, what triggers it, and how you can avoid acting on it in hurtful ways.

APPLICATION I

It's easier to understand how hostility makes children feel if we remember our own experiences. Discuss two times when you were the recipient of someone else's anger. Write down the strongest anger you can remember receiving from one of your parents and from your spouse or an adult friend and answer the questions on the following pages.

Experience with Parent:

1. What had you done to precipitate the anger?

2. Describe your parents' reactions. (What did they do or say, how did they look, etc.)

3. How did you feel about yourself after their outburst?

4. How did you feel toward your parents?

5. Did their anger help or hinder you and your relationship with them in the long term? How?

6. What would have been more helpful?

Experience with spouse or friend:

1. What had you done to precipitate the anger?

2. Describe the anger directed toward you by your spouse or friend.

3. How did you feel about yourself after the outburst?

4. How did you feel toward your spouse or friend?

5. Did their anger help or hinder you and your relationship with them in the long term? How?

6. What would have been more helpful?

PRACTICE I

Choose a time you have been angry at one of your children and answer the questions below.

Child's action or attitude:

1. Why did your child's action upset you so much?

2. How did your child react to your anger?

3. How do you think he felt about himself after receiving your anger?

4. How do you think he felt about you?

5. What good came out of your anger?

6. If any good came out of your anger, do you think it offset the negative feelings it created in your child? Why or why not?

7. How could you have handled the situation differently?

8. What might you have learned or how might you have grown through this situation?

PRACTICE II

When we lose our tempers with our children, it is usually because we are feeling helpless or because they have triggered one of our "anger buttons." Sometimes we become angry because we think our children should obey us perfectly or because they have made us look bad in public. Sometimes we lose our tempers because that's the way our parents raised us. But whatever the cause, *when we become angry we lose our sensitivity to our children and our ability to feel with them and support them*. With your spouse or a friend, talk about the things that seem to trigger your anger. As you talk, try to understand why you lose your temper and how you may need to grow in order to be a kinder, gentler parent. Write what you learn in the space below.

SCRIPTURE: A patient man has great understanding, but a quick-tempered man displays folly (Proverbs 14:29).

PRAYER/MEDITATION: Lord, make me sensitive to my children's tender feelings so that I can nurture them rather than attack them. Help me restrain my first angry inpulse so that I can model your loving discipline. And help me to find my own hurts and sensitive spots so you can bring healing into my life too.

POINTS FOR PARENTS
Covenant for Managing Angry Feelings

I commit myself to:

- discipline my children instead of punish them.
- correct my children before I reach my boiling point.
- count to ten (or ten thousand!) before I act or speak.
- talk things over with my spouse or friend.
- take a "time-out" before I discipline.
- understand why my child is acting like he is.
- not sweat the small stuff.
- give direct "I" messages instead of blaming, "you" messages.
- ask God how I can grow.
- be patient with myself and my children.

Reckless words pierce like a sword, but the tongue of the wise brings healing (Proverbs 12:18).

CHAPTER 11

Building Your Child's Self-Image

REVIEW

Your children's self-concepts are the keys to their emotional adjustment. The attitudes and feelings your children develop toward themselves will impact their entire personalities. Children with largely positive thoughts and feelings about themselves are happy and well-adjusted. They get along well with others and even find it easier to accept God's love and forgiveness. Children with poor self-concepts are prone to loneliness, anxiety, depression, and hostility. They have more relational problems and tend to struggle more in their relationships with God. Although your children's teachers, friends, siblings, and pastors will have significant influences on their attitudes and feelings about themselves, you will make the biggest impact. The three cornerstones of your children's self-esteem are:

- a sense of belonging, or a feeling of being loved.
- a sense of confidence in their ability to perform.
- a sense of worth or a feeling of being a good, valuable, or significant person.

APPLICATION I

With your spouse, a friend, or your study group, think of several experiences that build up or enhance a child's feelings of love, confidence, and worth. Then write down three suggestions for each of the three areas of need.

Love:

Confidence:

Worth:

APPLICATION II

Read the vignette below and answer the question that follows.

Jackie is a bright but rather shy twelve-year-old. She receives good grades in school and has two or three close friends. In spite of this, Jackie seems rather depressed. She watches TV excessively and doesn't appear to have much confidence in herself. Jackie has two sisters—one older and one younger. Her father has a demanding job, and her mother works only mornings so that she can be home when her girls return from school. Jackie's parents are very involved in their church, where they each serve on some important committees. They love their girls and help them with activities at school whenever they can.

What do you think might be the reason behind Jackie's rather poor self-concept? (You can refer to anything in this brief vignette, but you can also guess about other things that may account for Jackie's difficulty in feeling good about herself.)

APPLICATION III

Imagine an upstanding couple in your community who seem, from all outward appearances, to be fine parents. Despite that appearance, one of their children is quite depressed and the other is extremely unsure of himself and lacks confidence.

1. Make a list of several things these parents might be doing around the home that may be making their children feel absolutely terrible about themselves even though people who don't see inside the home might think it was an ideal family.

2. Even though the farthest thing from your mind is to make your children feel bad about themselves, do you notice that you do any of the things you listed above? If so, which ones?

3. Now let's say you have adopted the children from the above family. Make a list of five things you would do to help these children overcome their low self-esteem and develop positive feelings about themselves.

PRACTICE I

For three days during the next week, try to be especially sensitive to the sense of confidence in one of your children. Make a list of things that happen or things you do or say which might undermine this part of his or her self-esteem (i.e., criticisms, failures, overprotection, comparisons to a sibling, being beaten up by the neighborhood bully, etc.). Then list everything you notice that helps build up his confidence.

1. Experiences that hindered your child's sense of confidence or competence:

2. Experiences that strengthened your child's sense of confidence or competence:

PRACTICE II

For another three-day period, give careful attention to every experience that influences your child's feeling of being lovable.

1. Experiences that hindered your child's feeling of being loved:

2. Experiences that strengthened your child's feeling being loved:

PRACTICE III

When children are sad or depressed, they usually feel lonely, unworthy, or like failures. Pick a time when one of your children seemed depressed and discuss it below.

1. Describe her looks and feelings during this time of depression.

2. What do you think caused the depression?

3. Which self-concept needs were probably unmet or were being undermined?

4. What can you do in a similar situation to help her out of the depression?

5. Could you have done anything to prevent or minimize your child's discouragement ahead of time? If so, what?

SCRIPTURE: What is man, that you are mindful of him, the son of man that you care for him? You made him a little lower than the heavenly beings and crowned him with glory and honor (Psalm 8:4–5). Jesus said, "Let the little children come to me, and do not hinder them, for the kingdom of heaven belongs to such as these" (Matthew 19:14).

PRAYER/MEDITATION: Lord, you have given me the responsibility to let my children know how much you love them and how special they are to you and me. Help me show them they are deeply loved and special to you and me. And help me help them develop confidence in the abilities you have given them.

CHAPTER 12

How *Not* to Talk with Your Children About Sex

REVIEW

Children's attitudes about sex are shaped by their knowledge of the human body and by their most important relationships—their relationships with their parents. Even though society makes it difficult for children to learn good sexual attitudes and values, they will if they experience:

- a loving relationship with their same-sex parent (or parent substitute), so they grow up wanting to be like that person.
- a loving relationship with their opposite-sex parent (or parent substitute), so they grow up desiring to marry and have a loving relationship with a member of the opposite sex.
- an attitude of openness and naturalness in talking about the body and sexuality in the home.
- direct answers to questions about sex.
- calmness from their parents when parents find them exploring their bodies or sexually explicit materials.
- a wholesome attitude toward sex as a God-given gift.

APPLICATION I

Perhaps the best way to understand how children feel about their bodies and sex is to remember how you felt. Think of the time you felt most curious, confused, frightened, or guilty about your body and your sexuality and complete the following:

1. Describe the situation and how you felt.

2. How do you think your parents would have reacted if they knew what you were thinking, feeling, or doing?

3. What would have been helpful to you at that time?

APPLICATION II

We develop a lot of our feelings about sex from the way we were brought up.

1. Describe the way your parents seemed to think and talk about sex and the human body as you were growing up.

2. How did you feel about your body and your sexuality when you were an elementary-aged child?

3. How did you feel about your body and sexuality when you were a teenager?

4. How helpful were your parents in assisting you with your concerns about your sexuality? Give an example.

PRACTICE I

To help our children develop healthy sexual attitudes and values, we need to know precisely the values and attitudes we want them to develop. Discuss with your spouse, friend, or study group the sexual attitudes and values you want your children to develop. Then list your top seven goals.

1.

2.

3.

4.

5.

6.

7.

PRACTICE II

Our children's need for sexual information changes as they grow. If you are in a study group or class, break into smaller groups based on the ages of your children. Make a list of the specific facts of life or information about the human body your children need at their ages.

Age: What they should know:

PRACTICE III

Look for an opportunity to discuss some aspect of sexuality with one of your children this next week. Look for a natural way to engage your child in a conversation about the human body, sexuality, or sexual attitudes and values. They might spontaneously ask a question, or you may start a conversation around some experience they had or something they read or saw on TV. Then answer the following questions:

1. How did you feel the instant you started discussing sex with your child?

2. If you felt a little embarrassed or awkward, describe that feeling and tell why you think you felt that way.

3. How did your child seem to feel?

4. Make a list of some other experiences you might use in the future to initiate some natural conversations about sex with your children.

5. If you felt too embarrassed to talk freely about sex, you may need to do a little work to overcome some of your anxiety and shame. Here's a three-step method. First, go to a room by yourself and simply name every body part and sexual act. Next, practice an imaginary conversation with your child. Finally, role-play or rehearse a casual, open discussion of sex with your spouse, a friend, or a study group member. If you need to repeat it several times, do it. Then write out the difference in the way you felt when you began this exercise and how you feel now. If you still feel anxious or embarrassed, keep talking, practicing, and reading until you feel more relaxed and natural. How does it feel to overcome your negative reactions to talking about sex?

SCRIPTURE: So God created man in his own image, in the image of God he created him; male and female he created them (Genesis 1:27).

PRAYER/MEDITATION: Lord, I thank you that you make us male and female and that you created us to share physical and emotional intimacy. Help me bring up my children knowing that their bodies and their sexuality are wonderful gifts from you. And help me teach them to develop biblical values that will enable them to wait until marriage before they experience the sexual fulfillment you designed.

CHAPTER 13

Working Mothers:
Women in Two Worlds

REVIEW

Chapter 13 of *Help! I'm a Parent* discusses two tough questions facing mothers who work, or are considering working, outside the home. First, if you are a mother thinking about working outside the home, what should you consider? Here are five of the most important principles:

- All children need substantial amounts of time with their parents.
- Children especially need their mother during their first three years.
- Day care can be a good solution, but babies who spend more than twenty hours a week in nonmaternal care during their first year of life have a greater likelihood of insecure attachment to their mother and of being noncompliant and aggressive.
- By the time children reach three or four years of age, they are generally ready for day care centers, nursery schools or daytime babysitters.
- Every child is different. Some need for their mother to be available well into adolescence, while others do not.

Second, if you are a mother who is already working outside the home, how can you best handle the pressures you face? Here are some suggestions:

- Get help around the home.
- Consider job sharing, telecommuting, flexible schedules, and other creative alternatives.
- Make time for yourself.
- When you are with your children, give them your undivided attention.

APPLICATION I

If you are in a study group, list and compare the childhood experiences of those who had mothers working outside the home with those whose mothers remained at home. Write down four similarities and four differences.

Similarities:

Differences:

APPLICATION II

Three mothers in different situations are considering taking jobs outside the home. Alicia is the mother of two children under three years old. Her husband is a well-paid professional and she wants to continue her career. Dawn is the mother of a six-year-old who wants to earn enough money so she and her husband can purchase their first home. Irene is the mother of a newborn. Her husband has a good job, but they won't be able to afford a nice home in Southern California for several years unless Irene goes to work. Discuss the pros and cons of each of these mothers going to work outside the home and tell what decision you think you might make in a similar situation.

Alicia's situation:

Dawn's situation:

Irene's situation:

PRACTICE I

1. If you are working outside the home, list the four most difficult things about your situation, then discuss them with your husband, a friend, or your study group.

2. List several ways you have learned to balance your family and career responsibilities.

3. How do your children seem to feel about your working?

4. Have you noticed any changes in the way your children act or in the way they relate to you since you went to work?

PRACTICE II

1. Time is precious when you are a working mother. Select one thing you are going to do differently in the next week to be sure you are connecting well with your children.

2. At the end of the week, write down how it went.

3. List other steps you can take to meet your children's needs to spend time with you.

4. List three steps you can take to relieve yourself of excess pressure. Do one of them this week and write down how it helped you cope.

PRACTICE III

If you are married, go out to dinner with your husband to talk frankly about your struggles and feelings about being a mother and an employee. If you are a solo parent, do the same with a friend. Write down any encouragement you received, any offers of help from your husband, and any good ideas. Also, take time to write down your feelings after your dinner and discussion.

SCRIPTURE: A wife of noble character who can find? She is worth far more than rubies. . . . Her children arise and call her blessed (Proverbs 31:1, 28).

PRAYER/MEDITATION: Lord, help me to find that vital balance between meeting my children's needs and my own.

CHAPTER 14

A Perspective for Change

Well, we've come to the end. Or should we say the beginning? You have just finished a program designed to help you become more sensitive to your children's needs and feelings and to assist you in learning how to discipline effectively. Let's review your progress and look toward the future.

REVIEW

What are the four most helpful principles or techniques you have learned from this course?

1.

2.

3.

4.

List four changes you have seen in your attitudes toward your children or your understanding of them during this course.

1.

2.

3.

4.

Have you seen any specific changes in your children's behavior or in their feelings about themselves? If so, list them here.

PRACTICE I

1. List the areas in which you would like to see further growth in your children.

2. What will you need to do to help make that growth happen?

3. List three areas in which you want to keep growing as a person and as a parent.

4. What kind of help will you need in order to keep growing in these areas (e.g., have regular talks with your spouse or a friend, stick to your commitment, read other books, review this course, seek counseling, etc.)?

A FINAL WORD

Raising children is a big task, and we are all in a process of growth. There are no perfect parents! I hope this program has helped you learn some more effective ways of working with your children, but remember, it is only a beginning. Since our complete personalities are reflected in the way we parent, no book or set of techniques can turn us into "instant parents." My desire is that you keep growing. As you do, I pray that God will encourage you and enable you to "train up your children in the way they should go," so that you will have the assurance that "when they grow old they will not depart from it."

To check your progress, you might go to your calendar now and jot a note to review the progress you and your children have made in three to six months. Reading *Help! I'm a Parent* again at that time or analyzing your situation with another study group a year from now can also cement these principles in your mind.

SCRIPTURE: By wisdom a house is built, and through understanding it is established; through knowledge the rooms are filled with rare and beautiful treasures (Proverbs 24:3–4).

PRAYER/MEDITATION: Lord, I love the children you have entrusted to my care. Give me wisdom, understanding, and knowledge so that they may be established and their lives filled with treasures that come from knowing you and from seeing themselves as your valuable, special, deeply loved children.

Notes

Notes

Notes

Notes

Notes

Notes